Amos Fortune, Free Man

by
Elizabeth Yates

Teacher Guide

Written by
Debbie Triska Keiser

> **Note**
> The Puffin Books paperback edition of the book, © 1989, was used to prepare this guide. The page references may differ in other editions. Novel ISBN: 0-14-034158-7
>
> **Please note:** This novel makes references to heathenism, Christianity, and pagan practices. Please assess the appropriateness of this book for the age level, religious beliefs, and maturity of your students prior to reading and discussing it with them.

ISBN 1-58130-505-2

Copyright infringement is a violation of Federal law.

© 2004 by Novel Units, Inc., Bulverde, Texas. All rights reserved. be reproduced, translated, stored in a retrieval system, or transm (electronic, mechanical, photocopying, recording, or otherwise) from Novel Units, Inc.

Photocopying of student worksheets by a classroom teacher at a non-profit school who has purchased this publication for his/her own class is permissible. Reproduction of any part of this publication for an entire school or for a school system, by for-profit institutions and tutoring centers, or for commercial sale is strictly prohibited.

Novel Units is a registered trademark of Novel Units, Inc. Printed in the United States of America.

To order, contact your local school supply store, or—

PAPERBACKS - BMI BOUND BOOKS
TEACHER'S GUIDES - AUDIO-VISUALS
PO BOX 800 - DAYTON, N.J. 08810-0800
Toll Free Phone 1-800-222-8100
America's Finest Educational Book Distributor

Andrea M. Harris, Production Manager/Production Specialist
Kim Kraft, Product Development Manager/Curriculum Specialist
Suzanne K. Mammen, Curriculum Specialist
Heather Johnson, Product Development Specialist
Jill Reed, Product Development Specialist
Nancy Smith, Product Development Specialist
Pramilla Freitas, Production Specialist
Adrienne Speer, Production Specialist

Table of Contents

Summary 3

About the Author 3

Initiating Activities 4

Vocabulary Activities 5

Five Sections 16
   Each section contains: Summary, Vocabulary,
   Discussion Questions, and Supplementary Activities

Post-reading Discussion Questions 22

Post-reading Extension Activities 23

Assessment 24

Skills and Strategies

Thinking
Research, brainstorming, problem solving, creative thinking, critical thinking, compare/contrast, decision making, attributes, multiple perspectives, literary interpretation

Comprehension
Predicting, sequencing, foreshadowing, cause/effect, inference, summarizing, inferences

Vocabulary
Pictionary, word maps, prefixes, suffixes, defining, parts of speech

Writing
Personal writing, creative writing, poetry, reports, essays, plays

Listening/Speaking
Discussion, presentations, charades, debate, plays

Literary Elements
Literary analysis, story mapping, plot development, setting, character analysis, similes, metaphors

Across the Curriculum
Social Studies—developing maps, research, charting a course, time lines, cultures, historical references, religion, geography; Science—botany, animals, ecosystems; Math—measurement, money; Language—poetry, outlines, research, Old English vs. modern English; Music—composing lyrics; Art—illustrations, dramatization; Health—diet, nutrition

Summary

At-mun is born the son of a king in Africa in 1710. During a tribal celebration, his people are attacked by slave-traders, his father killed, and At-mun is taken captive. At the age of 15, he is transported to America on a slave ship and sold into slavery. At-mun is given the name Amos Fortune and learns to speak, read, and write through the study of the Bible. Throughout the remainder of his life, Amos uses his religious beliefs as a blueprint for righteous living. He holds his head high through persecution, poverty, and racism, and faces life's challenges with dignity, determination, and persistence. At almost 60 years of age, Amos Fortune buys his own freedom and starts his own tanning business. Through hard work and determination, he is able to purchase the freedom of four other slaves, buy land, build a home, and help others.

About the Author

Elizabeth Yates (1905–2001) grew up in the countryside of New York State. From an early age she wanted to write, and when she was 21 she went to New York City to make her dream a reality. She met and married William McGreal and soon moved to England, where she published her first book, *High Holiday*. She eventually moved back to the United States and continued her writing career, penning more than 40 books during her career. *Amos Fortune, Free Man*, perhaps her best-known book, won the Newbery Medal in 1951.

Background Information

Biblical references throughout the book point back to the major themes: determination, persistence, self-worth, and overcoming adversity. The name Amos means "burden-bearer" in Hebrew.

Genre: biography

Setting: 1700s; Africa, Massachusetts, and New Hampshire

Point of View: third person

Themes: determination, dignity, self-worth, power, adversity

Conflict: person vs. person, person vs. society

Date of first publication: 1950

Characters

Amos Fortune: born a prince of the At-mun-shi tribe in Africa in 1710; taken into captivity at age 15 and sold as a slave in Massachusetts; spends over half of his life as a slave; purchases his freedom and the freedom of several other slaves before he dies

Caleb Copeland: Quaker who purchases Amos when he first arrives in America; teaches Amos the cloth-making trade; Copeland family also teaches Amos reading, writing, and math

Ichabod Richardson: purchases Amos when Caleb Copeland dies; very religious and strict; teaches Amos the tanning trade

Lily: the first slave Amos frees; marries Amos; lives only one year in freedom

Lydia: the second slave Amos frees; lame; reminds Amos of his sister in Africa; lives only one year in freedom

Violet: the third slave Amos frees; third wife of Amos; mother of Celyndia; weaver

Celyndia: born into slavery; Violet's daughter, freed at age four with Violet

Initiating Activities

1. Previewing the book: Have students study the cover, consider the title, and read the synopsis on the back. Invite students to discuss what they read, then have them complete the Clue Search chart on page 6 of this guide.

2. Freewriting: Give students the following prompts. Ask them to choose one and freewrite about it for at least ten minutes.
    - A person should be free to choose his own religion.
    - Obstacles in life are both good and bad.
    - You can accomplish anything with determination.

3. Compare and Contrast: On page 45, the author states that most households believed in the adage: "Servants, be obedient to them that are your masters." The Copelands, however, believed that people should "Bear ye one another's burdens." Compare the two viewpoints and have students write a paragraph stating with which opinion they most agree.

4. Sequencing/Predicting: Select eight pivotal paragraphs from different parts of *Amos Fortune, Free Man*. Copy each paragraph onto several sentence strips. Cut each sentence apart and paper clip together. Clip the sentences in each paragraph together. Have students form eight teams. Distribute one paragraph to each team. Instruct teams to reconstruct each sentence first, then reconstruct the paragraph into a sensible order. Allow each team to glue its paragraph to a piece of chart paper. Have one representative from each team stand holding the chart. Invite the class to place the paragraphs in an order that makes sense. Have students compose essays predicting what the book will be about.

5. Prediction Chart: Have students set up a Prediction Chart (see pages 7–8 of this guide) to use as they read the book.

6. Character Web: Invite students to complete the Character Web (see pages 9–10 of this guide) as they read the book.

7. Story Map: Have students complete a Story Map of major events from the book as they read (see page 11 of this guide).

8. Reflection: Invite students to write to the following prompt:

    Imagine you are suddenly captured and forced to leave your homeland. After three months of harsh captivity, you arrive in a new country and are sold into slavery. You don't know the language, and you struggle to hold on to your past life.

    Write an essay that explains your feelings about your new life. Be sure to include thoughts on the following themes: self-worth, dignity, freedom, power, and adversity.

Vocabulary Activities

1. Have students create a crossword puzzle (see page 13 of this guide) using some of the vocabulary words from the book to assess prior knowledge.

2. Prefixes and suffixes: Encourage students to keep a record of the words they read in *Amos Fortune, Free Man* that have prefixes and suffixes attached. Have students determine whether the prefix or suffix always attaches the same meaning.

3. Categorization: Have students categorize the following vocabulary words into three groups: nouns, adjectives, and verbs. Encourage them to write each word on an index card or sticky note so they can move the words around more easily.

    mystic (3), seethed (9), conical (11), brandished (20), wharf (28), tallow (55), Sabbath (56), vex (56), robust (85), pilgrimage (100)

4. Vocabulary Boxes: Assign each student a vocabulary word and give each a pattern for a vocabulary cube (see page 12 of this guide). Before the cube is glued together, each face should contain one of the following: a vocabulary word, the definition of the word, illustration of the word, a synonym of the word, antonym of the word, a sentence using the word. Display the vocabulary boxes in the room.

5. Target Word Pictionary or Charades: Have students divide into two teams. Give one person a vocabulary word to draw or act out. Artists may not speak while drawing or acting. Have teammates guess the target words. Some suggested words from *Amos Fortune, Free Man* include:

    shackles (10), wharf (28), beckoning (38), merging (85)

6. Limericks: Have students select five vocabulary words. Challenge students to write a limerick using all five words. Here is an example:

    > There once was a *robust* horse,
    > That *reluctantly* veered off course.
    > His *master* mistaken,
    > 'Bout the *means* he had taken,
    > Being lost, he was full of *remorse*.

7. Synonym Survival: Have students stand in a circle. Say a recently studied vocabulary word and toss a ball (or other small object) to a student. The student has five seconds to say a synonym for the word given. One point is earned by the class for each correct answer. At the end of one turn, retrieve the ball and start again, saying the word and tossing the ball to another student. Set a time limit and challenge students to earn ten points by the end of the game. This game can be modified to require students to say antonyms.

Clue Search

Directions: Collect information about the book for each of the items. Write down the information and then make some predictions about the book.

Information Source	Information Provided
Dedication	
Title	
Cover Illustration	
Teasers on the cover	
Friends' recommendations	
Reviewers' recommendations/awards won	

Your predictions about the book:

Using Predictions

We all make predictions as we read—little guesses about what will happen next, how a conflict will be resolved, which details will be important to the plot, which details will help fill in our sense of a character. Students should be encouraged to predict, to make sensible guesses as they read the novel.

As students work on their predictions, these discussion questions can be used to guide them: What are some of the ways to predict? What is the process of a sophisticated reader's thinking and predicting? What clues does an author give to help us make predictions? Why are some predictions more likely to be accurate than others?

Create a chart for recording predictions. This could either be an individual or class activity. As each subsequent chapter is discussed, students can review and correct their previous predictions about plot and characters as necessary.

Use the facts and ideas the author gives.

Use your own prior knowledge.

Apply any new information (i.e., from class discussion) that may cause you to change your mind.

Predictions
_____
_____
_____
_____

Prediction Chart

What characters have we met so far?	What is the conflict in the story?	What are your predictions?	Why did you make these predictions?

Using Character Attribute Webs

Character attribute webs are simply a visual representation of a character from the novel. They provide a systematic way for students to organize and recap the information they have about a particular character. Attribute webs may be used after reading the novel to recapitulate information about a particular character, or completed gradually as information unfolds. They may be completed individually or as a group project.

One type of character attribute web uses these divisions:

- How a character acts and feels. (How does the character act? How do you think the character feels? How would you feel if this happened to you?)

- How a character looks. (Close your eyes and picture the character. Describe him/her.)

- Where a character lives. (Where and when does the character live?)

- How others feel about the character. (How does another specific character feel about the character?)

In group discussion about the characters described in student attribute webs, the teacher can ask for backup proof from the novel. Inferential thinking can be included in the discussion.

Character Web

Directions: Choose a character from the novel and complete the chart below. Cite evidence from the story as you fill in information.

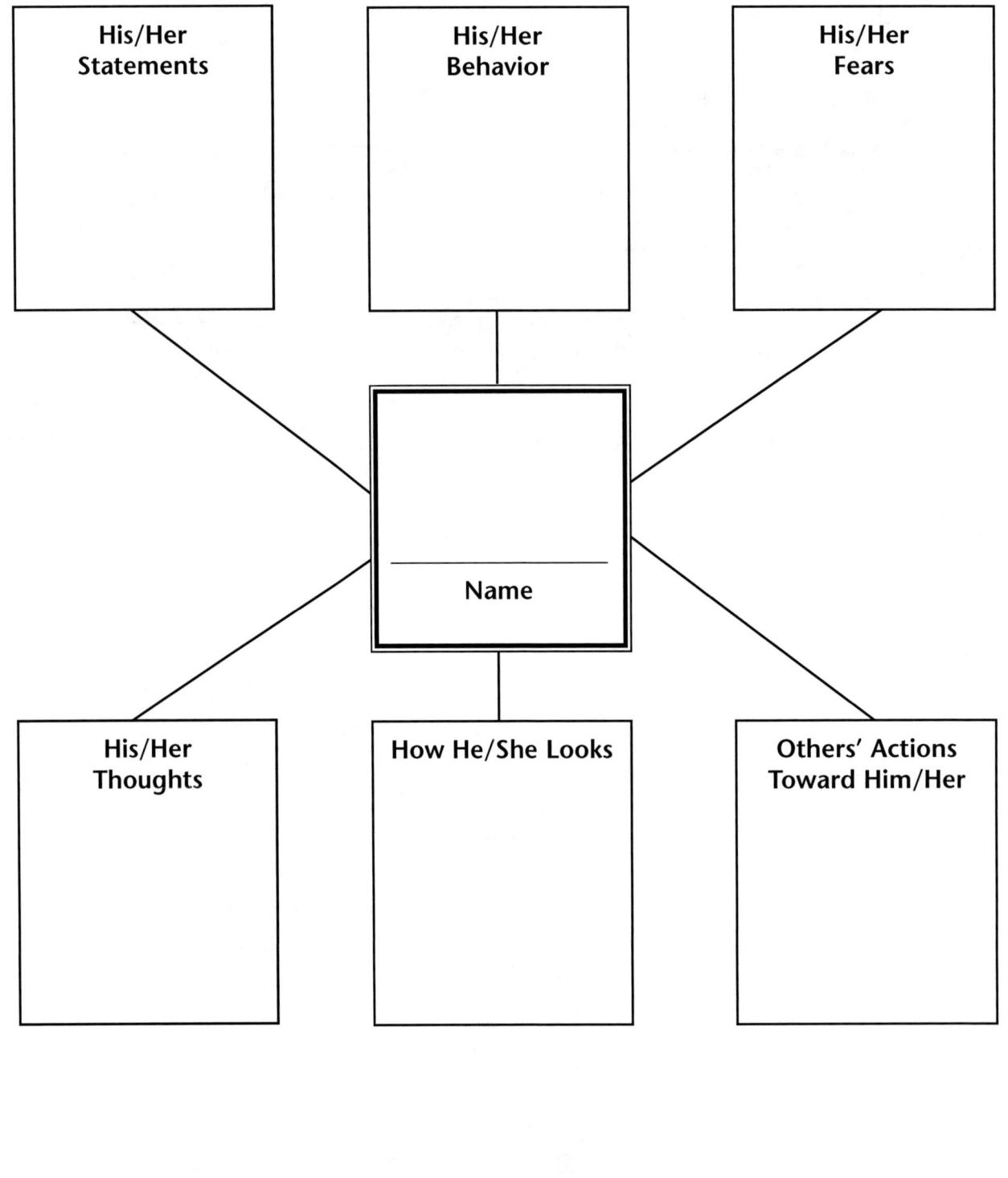

Story Map

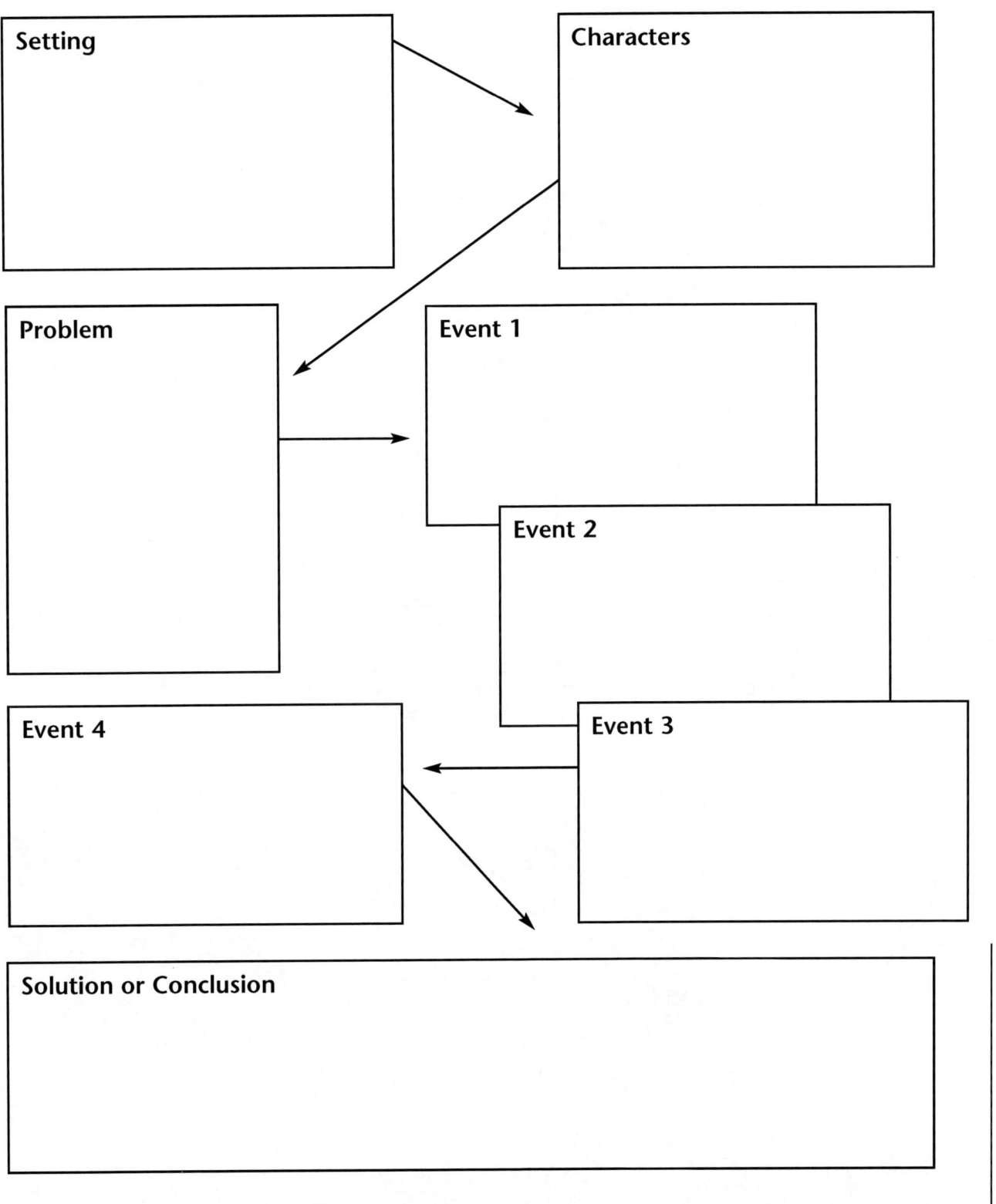

Vocabulary Cube Pattern

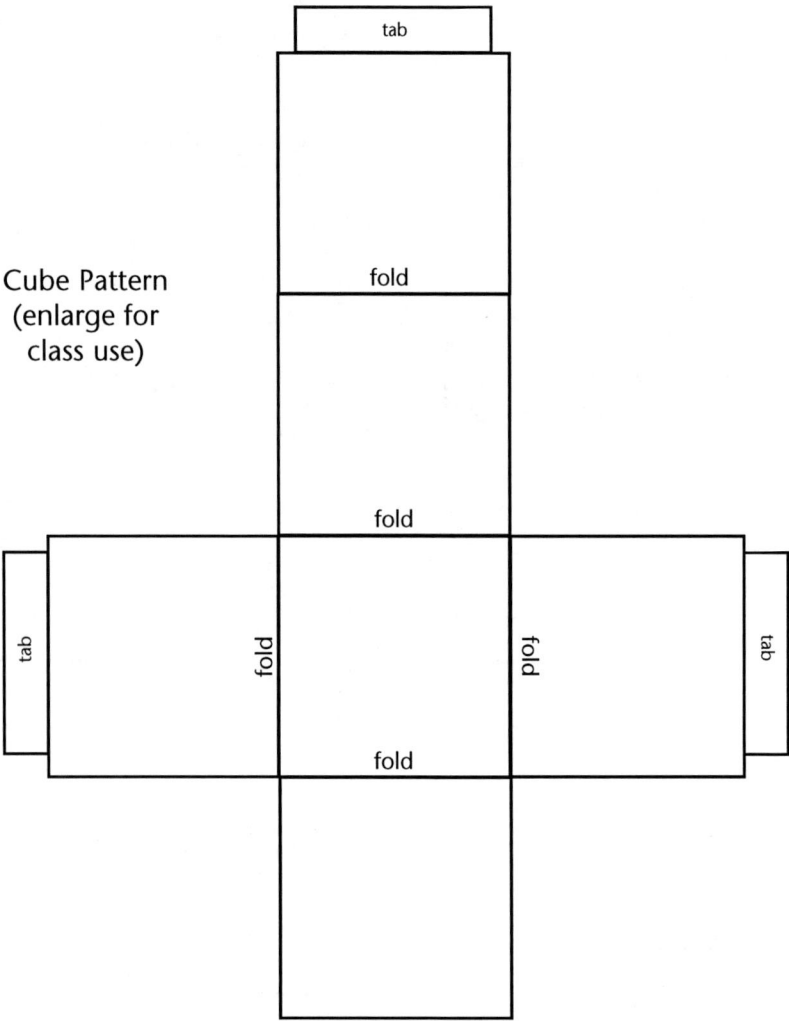

Crossword Puzzle

Directions: Select ten vocabulary words. Create a crossword puzzle answer key by filling in the grid below. Be sure to number the squares for each word. Blacken any spaces not used by the letters. Then, write clues to the crossword puzzle. Number the clues to match the numbers in the squares. The teacher will give each student a blank grid. Make a blank copy of your crossword puzzle for other students to answer. Exchange your clues with someone else and solve the blank puzzle s/he gives you. Check the completed puzzles with the answer keys.

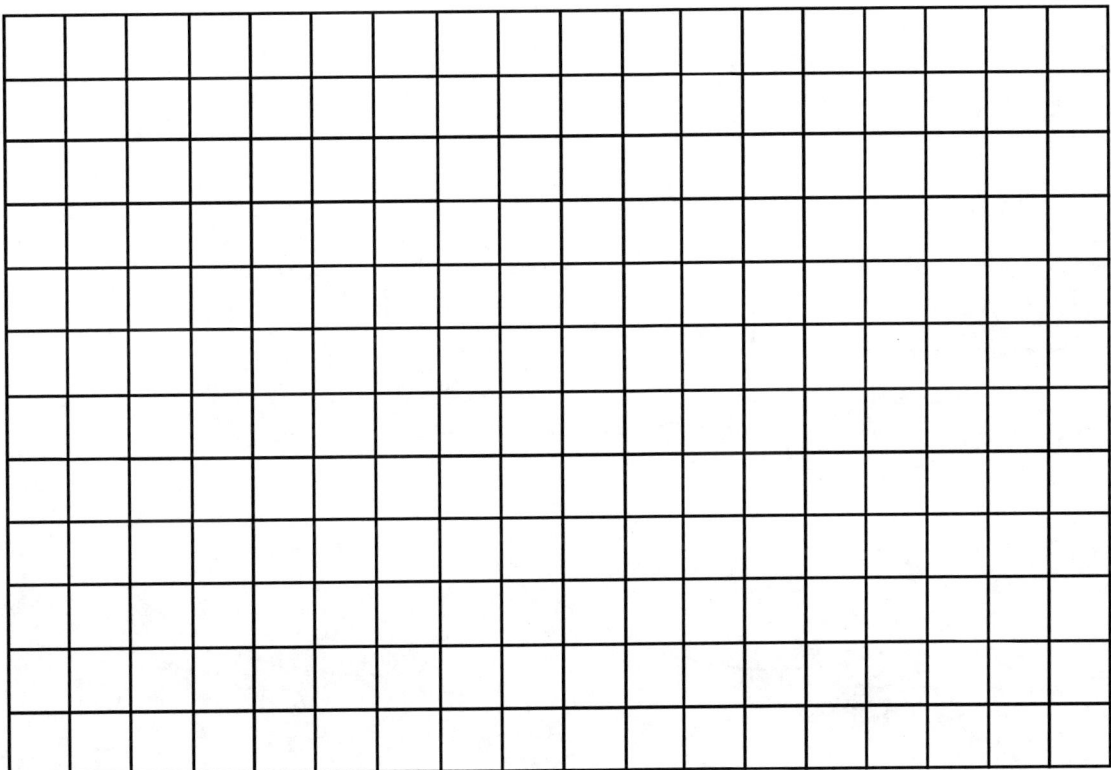

Venn Diagram

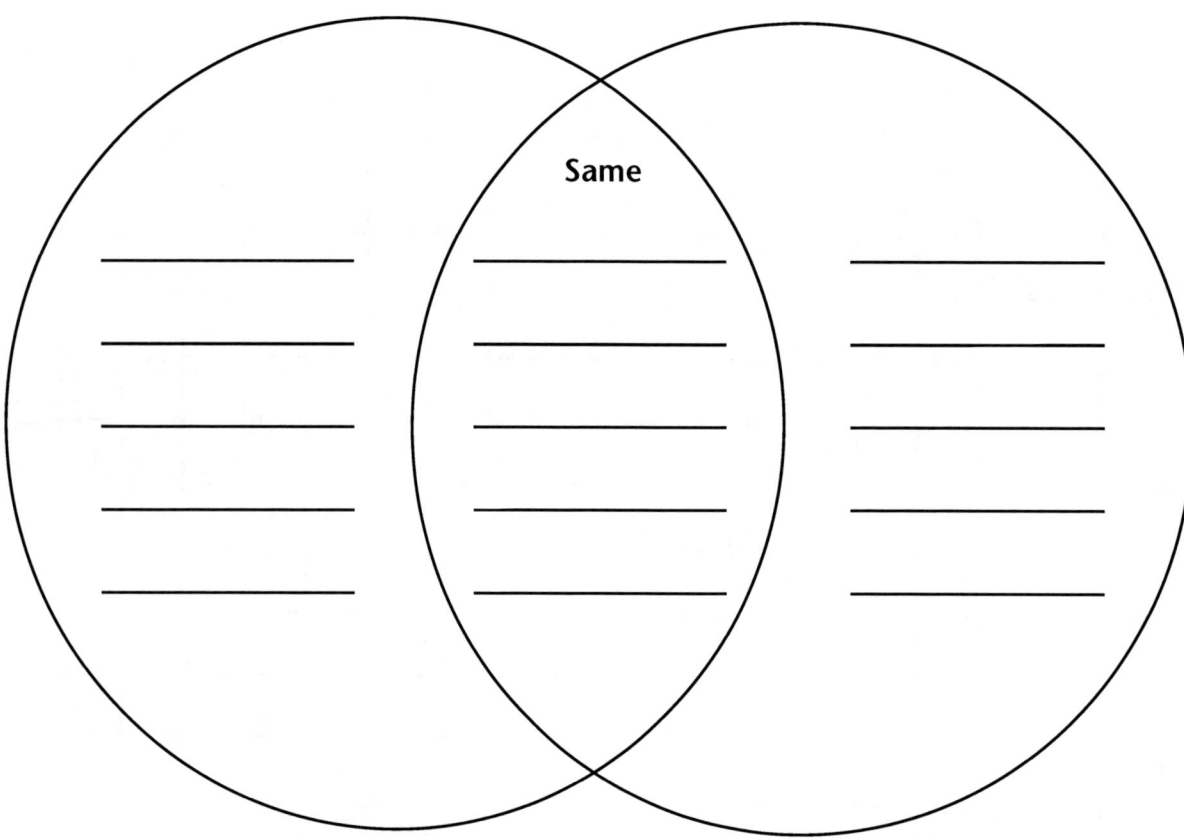

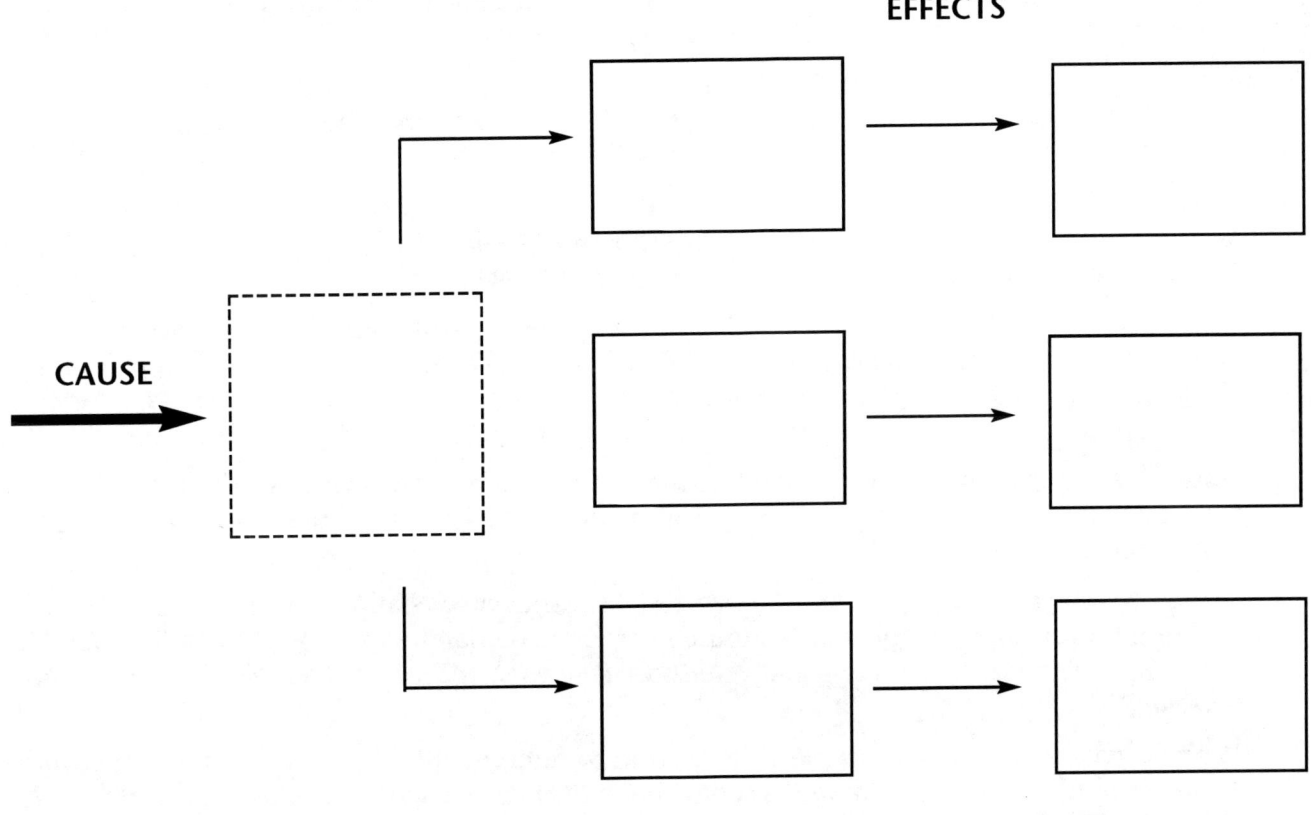

Africa 1725 & The Middle Passage, pp. 3–33

At-mun, a 15-year-old African prince, is captured by slave traders. He and his people endure extreme hardships as they are taken on a half-day journey to a river where they are loaded into canoes. Hours later they arrive where the river meets the ocean. After three weeks of living in unsanitary pits with little food or water, they board a sailing ship headed to America. For At-mun, the three-month journey ends in Boston. He is sold at a slave auction and renamed Amos Fortune.

Vocabulary
mystic (3)
obeisance (4)
pagan (5)
seethed (9)
shackles (10)
conical (11)
brandished (20)
shrewd (24)
wharf (28)
truculent (32)

Discussion Questions

1. According to the incantation on page 7 of the novel, what do the At-mun-shi people worship? *(nature)*

2. What does the old woman mean when she taps her head saying, "Not with this will he rule, but so," laying her hand on her heart? *(She is saying that At-mun has a good, kind heart, and he will rule his people well. p. 8)*

3. At the end of the first chapter, At-mun reminds his sister that she is a princess. Why do you think these are his parting words? *(Answers will vary. p. 12)*

4. What do you think At-mun is feeling as he leaves the familiarity of the jungle and journeys farther from his home than he had ever been before? *(responsibility for protecting and leading his people, anticipation, wonder, curiosity, fear of the unknown, p. 18)*

5. What does the author mean by the following, "To them it was a great bird sent for their deliverance and in his heart each one hailed it" (p. 20)? *(The At-mun-shi have been treated so badly up to this point that they hope to be delivered from their present situation into a better arrangement.)*

6. How were the tribesmen and women like merchandise after three weeks in the pit? *(They are treated as things to sell rather than as people who have emotional and physical needs and deserve respect. pp. 22–23)*

7. What does the author mean when she writes, "But the waves slapping against the ship had more meaning than the words shouted through the hatch" (p. 25)? *(The captives don't understand what the traders are shouting, but they know they are leaving their families and homeland.)*

8. Why do you think it is so important to At-mun to remember he is a king? *(Answers will vary. He understands his self-worth regardless of the external circumstances. This theme is repeated throughout the book. p. 27)*

9. According to his religious beliefs, is Caleb Copeland justified in purchasing a slave? *(Answers will vary. pp. 32–35)*

Supplementary Activities

1. Writing: There appears to be no written record of the At-mun-shi tribe in Africa except in the book *Amos Fortune, Free Man*. Based on the information provided in the first two chapters of the book, write an essay explaining why you think the tribe cannot be found.

2. Art: Draw a picture of the scene depicted on page 20, including the ship, holding areas, canoes, and captives.

3. Health: The captives were fed nothing but coconuts, coconut milk, bread, and water for three weeks. Research the nutritional value of a coconut and determine how long a person could survive on this diet.

4. Research: Use the Internet to learn more about the Middle Passage and the conditions of the captives as they were brought from Africa to America.

Boston 1725–1740 & Woburn 1740–1779, pp. 34–80

Caleb Copeland, the Quaker who purchased Amos, takes him home to live with his family. Mistress Copeland teaches Amos to speak, read, and write in English and to do math. Amos also learns to make cloth and adopts the family's religious beliefs. When Mr. Copeland dies suddenly, Amos is sold to help pay off debt. His new master, Ichabod Richardson, teaches him the tanning trade. At almost 60 years of age, Amos purchases his own freedom from the Richardson family and begins saving money to purchase Lily, one of his friends. Lily dies after one year of freedom, and Amos purchases Lydia. She also dies within a year.

Vocabulary
stalwart (34)
beckoning (38)
relinquished (40)
cipher (40)
admonition (45)
renowned (47)
immemorial (50)
tallow (55)
Sabbath (56)
vex (56)
oppression (72)

Discussion Questions

1. How does Celia know "At-mun" is not a sound, but a word in Amos' native language? *(Answers will vary. pp. 39–40)*

2. Why do you think the Bible is used for all schooling in the Copeland household? *(It likely is one of the few books in the house. Quakers are very stern in their religious faith and believe that all lessons in life should come from the Bible. pp. 40–41)*

3. How does Amos realize the word "king" refers to a person of worth? *(Answers will vary. As Roxanna reads from the Bible, Amos understands that every person is of value in God's eyes, regardless of color or station in life. pp. 41–42)*

4. Why doesn't Amos want to gain his freedom too soon? *(Amos has seen the difficulties experienced by former slaves who are not prepared to earn a living in a society where even free blacks lack status because of the color of their skin. p. 46)*

5. What kind of a man is Ichabod Richardson? *(stern, considered a good man, doesn't say much, wants everyone in his household to follow his religious beliefs, expects obedience, thinks he treats his slaves fairly, thinks of himself as a good Christian, pp. 53–55)*

6. What does the author mean when she writes, "The sun stood still over Africa, it was only in America that it moved" (p. 50)? *(In Amos' mind, his family, village, and homeland are set unchanging in one moment in time. Even though he has been in America for 15 years, he still looks for a 12-year-old girl with a limp.)*

7. What does the author mean when she writes, "It was not with his own people he felt at his best but with all men" (p. 56)? *(Amos is the same person whether at church or in the tanning yard. He treats every person, regardless of skin color, with care and respect. pp. 56–57)*

8. How does Amos compare his life to the life of Moses from the Bible? *(Amos is almost 60 years old when he finally experiences freedom. Moses lived to be 120 years old and was still mentally and physically strong. Amos feels that he is like Moses in that he has something to live for, is still strong, and will live for a long time. pp. 68–69)*

9. Why does Amos not argue with Mr. Bowers' price for Lydia? *(Amos does not want to barter over a human being. He also knows that as a black man, he has no leverage to question a white man. p. 79)*

10. **Prediction:** Will Amos' sister arrive on a boat from Africa? Explain your answer.

Supplementary Activities

1. Literary Devices: Skim the previous chapters, noting the author's use of similes and metaphors to illustrate Amos' thoughts and feelings. **Similes**—[Amos follows] "like an obedient dog" p. 38; "hope filtered through them like the sun through a dark day's clouds" p. 46; "a smile like the first rays of dawn" p. 48; "with eyes that like snuffed candles had no light in them" p. 63; **Metaphor**—"[the ship] was a great bird" p. 20

2. Mathematics: At the end of the third chapter Amos is sold for 62 pounds sterling. Research the value of that purchase price today.

3. Comparisons: Written and spoken English in the 1700s was much different than today's English. Rewrite the letter granting Amos his freedom from pages 64–65 of the novel in today's English.

4. History: Read the Declaration of Independence. Write an essay explaining how the words of the document did not pertain to slaves.

5. Research: Locate information about the Boston Tea Party. Research the effects the rebellion had on slaves.

Journey to Keene 1779 & The Arrival at Jaffrey, pp. 81–108

Amos has been a free man for ten years. He looks for a place to resettle and purchases the freedom of Violet and her four-year-old daughter, Celyndia. The family arrives in Jaffrey, New Hampshire, with dreams of building a home and starting a tanning business but are asked to leave. The town eventually makes them feel welcome, and Amos is allowed to start his business on Parson Ainsworth's land.

Vocabulary

merging (85)
robust (85)
consigned (86)
frugally (94)
dolefully (99)
pilgrimage (100)
shrewdly (102)
endeavor (102)

Discussion Questions

1. What does the author mean when she writes of Amos, "A strange thing freedom was, he thought, with its side of shadow as well as of light"? *(Amos is free of household cares and domestic ties, but he longs for a woman to share his life with. p. 82)*

2. Why is Amos especially excited about Celyndia's freedom? *(He wants her to grow up free so she will never feel that slavery's social barriers apply to her. pp. 82–83)*

3. What important truth does Amos understand about the inequality between white men and free black men? *(Even when he is free, a black man does not have the same rights as a white man and therefore must be agreeable so he doesn't draw undue attention to himself. p. 86)*

4. What does Amos notice about Samuel George that helps him negotiate a price for his tanning services? Does Samuel George recognize that Amos is doing him a favor? *(Samuel George is slow to count out the money he owes. Amos also notices that Samuel is a large man, and his go-to-Meeting clothes haven't been worn in a while; Samuel thinks of Amos as being childlike rather than recognizing that Amos took the clothes as much to help Samuel as himself. pp. 87–89)*

5. Amos sets out with an ax and a bag of beans as his prized possessions when he, Violet, and Celyndia leave for the trip to Jaffrey. What would you take as your prized possessions for survival and why? *(Answers will vary. pp. 94–95)*

6. Why do you think Violet's favorite color is white? *(Answers will vary. In her mind, white stands for freedom, richness, and everything good. p. 96)*

7. What does being a king mean to Amos? *(Answers will vary. Amos knows that he was born to be a king in Africa, but he believes that living a God-centered, righteous life makes him a king in his present circumstances. p. 98)*

8. What is the "usual warning" Amos receives upon his arrival in Jaffrey? *(The town constable is obligated to let any black settlers know that the town won't be responsible for caring for the family should they become destitute. pp. 100–104)*

9. What emotions do you think Amos is feeling as he, Violet, and Celyndia spend their first night in Jaffrey? *(elation, anticipation, peace, contentment, p. 108)*

Supplementary Activities
1. Map Skills: Locate on a map all of the places where Amos lived. Chart his route to each destination, noting geographical features such as mountains, lakes, and rivers. Then create a time line showing when he made each move.

2. Art: On the Internet, research how to make a cornhusk doll and then make one.

3. Research: Compile a list of ten facts about Monadnock Mountain to share with the class.

Hard Work Fills the Iron Kettle 1781–1789 & Amos on the Mountain, pp. 109–145

Amos and Violet work hard to establish the tanning business and to build their home. Amos again feels the need to be charitable. Violet does not like the family he wishes to help because they don't try to help themselves. Violet hides the money in the kettle, and Amos climbs Mount Monadnock to pray for an answer as to what he should do about helping the Burdoo family. Amos finally realizes his dream of owning his own land.

Vocabulary
abode (110)
pliable (112)
convex (117)
concave (117)
impervious (118)
bevy (125)
feign (129)
excavate (130)
stifled (138)
summit (140)

Discussion Questions
1. Why does Celyndia still question whether she can go and do as she pleases? *(She has been a slave since birth and has never known freedom. pp. 110–111)*

2. Amos leads a truly happy life. Where does this happiness come from? What does he see as being his life's purpose? *(Answers will vary. p. 115)*

3. Violet sees Amos as climbing a mountain in his mind. What does she mean by this? *(Answers will vary. pp. 115–116)*

4. Why is there a separate place for blacks to worship in the church? *(The white population does not view the black population as equal, no matter how well educated, successful in business, or helpful to the community. p. 120)*

5. Why do you think it took so long for Amos to be invited to join the church he attended in Jaffrey? *(Answers will vary. p. 122)*

6. What kind of person is Lois Burdoo? *(She is dependent on the charity of others for her survival. She does not seem to be able or willing to provide for herself or her family. p. 127)*

7. Compare and contrast Lois and Violet. *(Answers will vary.)*

8. Do you think Violet is right in not wanting to help the Burdoo family? Explain your answer. *(Answers will vary. p. 132)*

9. Why does Violet keep her eyes on the mountain as she tells Amos about hiding the kettle? *(Answers will vary. She looks to the mountain for the strength to stand up for something in which she believes. p. 134)*

10. What, besides the mountain, gives Violet the strength to stand up to Amos? *(She knows Amos repeatedly sets his own dreams aside for the sake of others. She speaks for the part of Amos that needs to see his dreams fulfilled. p. 135)*

11. Who makes the better argument for what should be done with the money? *(Answers will vary. pp. 134–136)*

12. Violet says, "You'll do more for them all by giving work to the boys than by giving money to Lois" (p. 136). What does she mean by this? *(It will be better to teach the boys a skill they can use to support themselves and their family than to just give them money.)*

13. Why does Amos go to the mountain to pray about the money situation? *(He sees the mountain as being closer to God. He is troubled and needs answers. pp. 138–141)*

Supplementary Activities

1. Research/Compare and Contrast: Research the process for tanning leather today. Then read the steps for tanning leather in the 1700s (pp. 117–119). Compare and contrast the processes using the Venn diagram found on page 14 of this guide.

2. Science/Art: Locate pictures and information about lilac, tea rose, japonica, and lily-of-the-valley flowers. Write a descriptive paragraph or draw a picture of what Violet's garden might look like.

3. Writing: Write about a time when you chose to do something you believed in even though you weren't sure if you were right or wrong. How did the event turn out?

Vocabulary
indentured (147)
illiteracy (149)
bolster (150)
indigent (150)
despatched (153)
reverie (157)
ebbing (169)
affronts (171)
pittance (172)
notion (176)

Auctioned For Freedom & Evergreen Years 1794–1801, pp. 146–181

Amos finds a way to help the Burdoo family after all. He is paid by the town to take care of Polly and hires two of her brothers to work for him. He also takes on an apprentice to help with the workload. Amos realizes his life is short and draws up a will. In the will he leaves his worldly possessions to Violet and Celyndia and a large sum of money to the church and school. The money he leaves to the school creates a fund that is still in existence today.

Discussion Questions

1. Why do you think Amos feels that he owes Violet? *(Answers will vary. p. 148)*

2. Do you think the Public Vendue was a good plan for towns to care for their needy in the late 1700s? Explain your answer. *(Answers will vary. p. 150)*

3. How does a mountain give someone strength? *(Answers will vary. p. 153)*

4. What does the mountain represent in this book? *(strength, God, courage, determination, obstacles to overcome, the path to heaven, etc. p. 153)*

5. Amos says, "Wings can't grow without a little suffering." What does he mean by this? *(Going through difficult times often makes a person stronger and wiser. p. 156)*

6. Why do you think Polly stares off all the time? *(Answers will vary. p. 158)*

7. What does Violet see in Amos' character that causes her to love him even more after Polly dies? *(He is so unselfish and always thinking of others before himself. p. 161)*

8. What does Amos mean when he says, "It does a man no good to be free until he knows how to live, how to walk in step with God" (p. 162)? *(Amos believes that true freedom comes from living a righteous, God-centered life and helping others.)*

9. What does it mean that Amos will account to Ath-mun when they meet together at the Jordan? *(Amos devoted his life to helping helpless people in memory of his sister. pp. 169–170)*

10. How can hate be like a burning mountain? *(Answers will vary. Fire can consume everything in its path. Hate can take over a person's thoughts and actions and can destroy any joy in a person's life. pp. 172–173)*

11. Summarize Amos' will. Do you agree with how he distributed his money and possessions? *(He is leaving his land and possessions to Violet and Celyndia, donating money for a silver communion service to the church, and is leaving a sizeable amount of money to the school to educate both white and black children. Answers will vary. pp. 177–179)*

12. What is different about the money Amos saves in the stone crock? Why do you think he saves that money separately from the money he earns tanning hides? *(Answers will vary. p. 179)*

13. What does Amos hope to accomplish through his donations to the church and school? *(He hopes for equality between the black and white populations. pp. 179–180)*

Supplementary Activities

1. History/Research: Research the Amos Fortune Forum. It was founded in 1946 to continue the fund he started in the school. Write a report telling what you learn about the fund and its purpose.

2. History: The separation Amos felt between blacks and whites only got worse through the years. The Supreme Court tackled the problem in the famous court case *Brown v. Board of Education*. Find books or articles to read about this historic court case and discuss your findings with your class.

3. Compare and Contrast: In Amos' day, townspeople worked together to take care of those in need. Today we have many types of aid in the form of shelters, low rent housing, welfare, etc. Choose a public program and compare it to the Public Vendue system set up in towns during the 1700s. Write an essay describing each kind of aid and explain which you think is most effective.

Post-reading Discussion Questions

1. How does Amos Fortune show courage and determination throughout his life?
2. How do Amos' religious beliefs affect the choices he makes throughout his life?
3. What does Amos mean when he says, "It does a man no good to be free until he knows how to live" (p. 162)?
4. Why is it important to Amos to be educated and free?
5. What does Amos mean when he talks about his "promised land"?
6. Why does Celyndia cry when she realizes she is free to go where she pleases?
7. How is Amos' character revealed as he purchases his own freedom and then the freedom of others?
8. How is Amos affected when he sees his reflection in the polished tin? Why does he feel this way?
9. What do you think is the climax of the story? Cite references from the book to support your answer.
10. How do you think Amos' experiences as a prince prepared him for his experiences as a freed slave?
11. How does Amos' attitude affect those who know him? Cite references from the book.
12. For what kind of person does Amos have a soft spot in his heart? Cite references from the book to support your answer.
13. Why do you think Amos Fortune is a fitting name for the boy who was once a prince? Explain your answer.
14. How is Amos Fortune like Monadnock Mountain? Explain your answer.

Post-reading Extension Activities

1. In a small group, play "What's My Word?" Write vocabulary words from *Amos Fortune, Free Man* on sticky notes or index cards. Stick or pin one word to the back of each student. Students are not allowed to know what word is on their backs. Give students a list of all the vocabulary words from the book. Students must ask "yes or no" questions of their peers to discover the word they are wearing. The first person to correctly determine the word he or she is wearing is the winner. Mix the cards, restick them, and play again.

2. Write about how the book would have been different if the protagonist had been a female trying to make a life in the 1700s instead of a male.

3. Read a book about Harriet Tubman or another person who worked diligently to free slaves. Use the Venn Diagram on page 14 of this guide to compare and contrast that individual with Amos Fortune.

4. Research Quaker laws for the Sabbath.

5. If you had to choose ten scenes of significance from the book, which would they be and why? Draw a series of ten pictures and write a paragraph telling how each picture is important to Amos' life.

6. Change the words to a familiar nursery rhyme to retell the story of Amos Fortune.

7. Select one chapter from the book to dramatize or illustrate. Create a script, cast parts, and arrange for props. Present your play to the class.

8. Locate other books written by Elizabeth Yates. Read the synopses of several books. Why do you think Yates felt compelled to write this book? Write an essay defending your answer.

9. Write a poem that tells about Amos Fortune's sense of self-worth. How does his confidence in himself shine throughout the book?

10. Reread the chapter titled "Auctioned for Freedom." Create a list of the conflicts and resolutions from this chapter.

11. How might the book have been different if Amos Fortune had not been born a prince? Write an essay citing references from the book to support your answer.

12. Check out a book about Sojourner Truth from the library. Create a Venn diagram comparing this book to *Amos Fortune, Free Man*.

Assessment for *Amos Fortune, Free Man*

Assessment is an ongoing process. The following ten items can be completed during the novel study. Once finished, the student and teacher will check the work. Points may be added to indicate the level of understanding.

Name _____ Date _____

Student	Teacher	
_____	_____	1. Discuss the Post-reading Discussion Questions on page 22 of this guide with a partner. Choose one question to answer in a multi-paragraph essay.
_____	_____	2. Write an essay about freedom. Why is freedom important?
_____	_____	3. Revisit the predictions you made at the beginning of the book and check your accuracy.
_____	_____	4. Choose one of the Post-reading Extension Activities on page 23 of this guide to complete.
_____	_____	5. Create a Venn diagram comparing Amos Fortune to Monadnock Mountain.
_____	_____	6. Write a persuasive composition stating what you believe is the climax of the book. Cite specific quotes to support your answer.
_____	_____	7. Create a cause-and-effect chart (see page 15 of this guide) about one major event in the book. Then write a paragraph telling how the book would have changed if the event had never occurred.
_____	_____	8. Create a flow chart that shows the major events in the story as they occur.
_____	_____	9. Consider other books you have read. Create a list of characters from other books who exhibit the same qualities as Amos Fortune: determination, pride, persistence, patience, etc.
_____	_____	10. Amos frequently looks to the mountain for strength. From what do you gain your strength? Write an essay telling about a supportive person or comforting thing that gives you strength to do difficult things.